Building Language Arts Skills Workbook

American Literature

Shoreview, MN

Table of Contents

Unit 1

Unit 2

Unit 3

Unit 4

Unit 5

Unit 6

Unit 7

The History of Plymouth Plantation

Directions Write the answers to these questions. Use complete sentences.

Literary Terms

1. Certain settings help to create a specific mood. Think about books or movies that you have read or seen. Write the titles of two books or movies. Describe the setting of each. Tell how the setting affects the mood of each story.

_____

_____

_____

_____

Reading on Your Own

2. As you read the selection from *The History of Plymouth Plantation,* list those words that help to describe the setting. Use those words to create a diary entry from the point of view of one of the Pilgrims who just landed in America.

_____

_____

_____

Grammar Check

3. Rewrite the following sentence adding adjectives to the sentence: *The Pilgrims arrived to shore after traveling on the ocean for months.* What effect do the adjectives have on the sentence?

_____

_____

_____

_____

Speaking

4. With a partner, create a conversation between two Pilgrims who have just landed in America. Keep in mind Bradford's description of the land and people. Practice your conversation. Then present it with your partner in front of the class. Write how you think the conversation worked.

_____

_____

_____

_____

_____

_____

Listening

5. Listen as your classmates present their short conversations from the Speaking activity above. What elements from Bradford's diary did the students include in their presentations? Discuss each group's performance.

_____

_____

_____

_____

_____

_____

To My Dear and Loving Husband

Directions Write the answers to these questions. Use complete sentences.

Literary Terms

1. Practice creating metaphors about love. For example, to what can love be compared? Write three of your own metaphors about love.

_____

_____

_____

Reading on Your Own

2. Consider the images Bradstreet uses to appeal to the reader's senses. What senses does she use? Create another image she could have used to express her love. Write this image about one of the senses Bradstreet has not already used.

_____

_____

_____

Grammar Check

3. Rewrite the following lines to create a parallel structure:

• To run, shopping, and swimming are my favorite things to do.

• I will always remember my dog for his playful manner, that he had warm and caring eyes, and his chocolate brown fur.

How does the parallel structure affect each sentence?

_____

_____

_____

_____

Speaking

4. Replace the words at the ends of Bradstreet's lines with synonyms, so that the poem no longer has rhyming couplets. Read the poem aloud with its new words. Do you prefer the original poem or the revised poem? Explain.

_____

_____

_____

_____

_____

_____

_____

Listening

5. Rewrite the poem in prose form. First, read the original poem aloud to a partner. Then, read the poem written in prose form aloud. How does the poem sound different when read without line breaks? Which way do you prefer? Explain.

_____

_____

_____

_____

_____

_____

_____

Poor Richard's Almanack

Directions Write the answers to these questions. Use complete sentences.

Literary Terms

1. What pen name would you use as a writer? Create a pen name and write it below. Then explain why you chose this name.

_____

_____

_____

_____

Reading on Your Own

2. As you read the selection from *Poor Richard's Almanack*, which piece of advice do you feel is most relevant to today? Why?

_____

_____

_____

_____

_____

Grammar Check

3. Write three sentences using at least two pronouns in each sentence. Do not repeat a pronoun once you have used it. Circle each pronoun.

_____

_____

_____

_____

_____

_____

Speaking

4. Choose the aphorism you like best from *Poor Richard's Almanack*. Decide whether you agree or disagree with the aphorism. Write a short paragraph using examples from your life that show the aphorism to be true or false. Read your paragraph to your class.

_____

_____

_____

_____

_____

_____

_____

_____

_____

Listening

5. Listen carefully to your classmates' paragraphs. Decide how well each speaker proves that the aphorism is either true or false. In addition, do they speak clearly and at a good rate? Do they make eye contact? Write down suggestions for the speakers and then share these with them.

_____

_____

_____

_____

_____

The American Crisis, Number 1

Directions Write the answers to these questions. Use complete sentences.

Literary Terms

1. What do you think are the advantages of writing in the form of a pamphlet? What are the disadvantages? Describe when you think a pamphlet would be a good form of writing to use.

_____

_____

_____

_____

_____

_____

Reading on Your Own

2. As you read Thomas Paine's *The American Crisis*, list the words that help to establish a certain tone. What is the overall tone of the passage?

_____

_____

_____

_____

_____

Grammar Check

3. Identify which of the three sentences below incorrectly uses *their* or *there*. Rewrite the sentence correctly on the lines below.

- *There* was a man named George Washington who fought hard for America.
- "I believe *their* is still hope," announced the brave man.
- The troops quickly packed up *their* gear when they heard the enemy coming.

_____

_____

_____

4. Write one sentence using both *there* and *their* correctly within the sentence.

_____

_____

_____

Speaking and Listening

5. Use what you have learned about Valley Forge and the winter of 1776. Create a conversation between two soldiers living during the time. Perform the dialogue in front of the class. As you listen to your classmates, identify facts from the time period included in the conversation. Write the facts on the lines below.

_____

_____

_____

_____

Wouter Van Twiller

Directions Write the answers to these questions. Use complete sentences.

Literary Terms

1. Write a brief physical description of one of your favorite characters in a book or movie. Use exaggeration in your description.

_____

_____

_____

_____

Reading on Your Own

2. As you read, list those words that help you to create a mental picture of Wouter Van Twiller. Use a dictionary or thesaurus to come up with a synonym for each word. Rewrite a short description of Wouter Van Twiller using the synonyms. How does the new description compare with the original?

_____

_____

_____

_____

_____

Grammar Check

3. For each of the following sentences, label each noun as abstract (A) or concrete (C). Also circle any proper nouns.

_____ Jim went to the park and then to the store.

_____ Love is the strongest emotion.

_____ Alice believes wisdom is more important than bravery.

_____ The dog ran across the street.

Speaking

4. Pair up with another student. One student is a journalist from a magazine holding a Person of the Year contest. The other is a supporter of Wouter Van Twiller. The journalist should ask questions to see if Twiller should be Person of the Year. Use specific details from the text to form questions and responses. Write your questions below.

_____

_____

_____

_____

_____

_____

_____

Listening

5. Listen to the interviews between the journalists and supporters of Wouter Van Twiller. What details from the text were included in the interviews? Did the supporters successfully convince the journalists that Twiller should be Person of the Year?

_____

_____

_____

_____

_____

_____

American Indian Poetry

Directions Write the answers to these questions. Use complete sentences.

Literary Terms

1. Write four sentences of your own using personification.

_____

_____

_____

_____

_____

_____

Reading on Your Own

2. As you read, notice some of the similar ideas in the poems. Why do you think these similarities exist?

_____

_____

_____

Grammar Check

3. Shorten the following sentence without changing the meaning: *There was a small man sitting on the bench without anyone next to him.* Explain the differences in the two sentences. Which sentence do you feel is more powerful?

_____

_____

_____

_____

_____

Speaking

4. After researching an American Indian nation, meet with other classmates who researched a different nation. Discuss with classmates the similarities and differences of the groups based on the research. Write some of the similarities and differences on the lines below.

_____

_____

_____

_____

_____

Listening

5. As you listen to your group members, record important information about each Indian nation. Write down such things as the group's name, location, food, customs, and important people and events. Use the information to prepare your slideshow presentation for the Listening and Research activity in your textbook.

_____

_____

_____

_____

The Origin of Plumage

Directions   Write the answers to these questions. Use complete sentences.

Literary Terms

1. Ask a family member or friend to recall a myth that he or she has heard. Summarize the myth below. Does it seem to fit the definition of a myth? Explain.

   _____

   _____

   _____

   _____

   _____

   _____

   _____

Reading on Your Own

2. Using a thesaurus, look up synonyms for the words *origin* and *plumage*. After you read "The Origin of Plumage," write a different title using the synonyms you found. Which title do you like better for the story? Why?

   _____

   _____

   _____

   _____

   _____

   _____

   _____

Grammar Check

Add commas where they belong to separate the introductory word or phrase in the following sentences.

3. After the long night in the desert they were ready to go back home.

4. However I do not think we have enough paper plates for everyone.

Speaking and Listening

5. With a partner, read "The Origin of Plumage" aloud. Then answer this question together: What qualities does a myth have that allow it to be passed along orally?

   _____

   _____

   _____

   _____

   _____

   _____

   _____

The Black Cat

Directions Write the answers to these questions. Use complete sentences.

Literary Terms

1. How would the story be different if it were written in a point of view other than first person? Would it be as powerful? Why or why not?

_____

_____

_____

_____

Reading on Your Own

2. Analyze the predictions you made before reading "The Black Cat." What predictions were correct? What surprised you about the short story?

_____

_____

_____

Grammar Check

3. Find a sentence from Poe's "The Black Cat" that uses dashes. Remember that a dash is used to show a broken or unfinished thought, whereas a hyphen joins two words together. Write the sentence below and explain how the dashes add to the meaning of the sentence.

_____

_____

_____

_____

Speaking

4. With a partner, write a short conversation between the narrator's wife and one of her friends concerning her husband. Use details from the story in the conversation. Then, present the conversation to your class. Write about how this added to your understanding of the story.

_____

_____

_____

_____

_____

_____

_____

_____

Listening

5. Listen as groups present their conversations between the narrator's wife and friend. How does each group interpret the wife's feelings? What details from the text are in each presentation?

_____

_____

_____

_____

Annabel Lee

Directions Write the answers to these questions. Use complete sentences.

Literary Terms

1. The rhyme helps to create the rhythm of this poem. How would the rhythm be affected by a different rhyme scheme? Explain.

_____

_____

_____

Reading on Your Own

2. Do you agree with the way Poe has broken the poem into stanzas? Would you have divided the poem differently? Explain.

_____

_____

_____

_____

Grammar Check

3. Write two sentences of your own that use the dash to show a broken or unfinished thought. Follow the style that Poe uses in "The Black Cat" and "Annabel Lee."

_____

_____

_____

_____

_____

Speaking

4. Read "Annabel Lee" aloud. Where in the poem do you feel you need to pause? Where do you adjust the speed of your voice? Practice reading the poem aloud to capture the emotion. Then read the poem to your classmates.

_____

_____

_____

_____

_____

_____

_____

Listening

5. Listen to your classmates read "Annabel Lee" aloud. Where do you think the narrator might be when he is speaking in the poem? What words would you use to describe the narrator's state of mind while he is speaking?

_____

_____

_____

_____

_____

_____

Unit 1 Review

Directions Write the answers to these questions. Use complete sentences.

Literary Terms

1. Choose a character from one of the selections in this unit. Then write a sentence using one of these types of figurative language: metaphor, exaggeration, or personification.

_____

_____

_____

Reading on Your Own

2. Read the Unit 1 Summary. Then write a description of each of the four styles of literature in your own words.

_____

_____

_____

_____

_____

Grammar Check

3. The different forms of the infinitive *to be* are very important when creating metaphors. Some forms of *to be* include *am, is, are, was,* and *were.* Change the following similes into metaphors using a form of *to be*. Write the new sentences on the lines provided.

He weighs as much as a horse.

_____

_____

She runs as fast as a roadrunner.

_____

_____

Speaking

4. Choose one of the selections listed in the Unit 1 Summary. Read the summary. Then choose three or four important details to remember about this selection. Form a group with students who chose different selections. Discuss the important points of each selection with your group members.

_____

_____

_____

_____

_____

_____

_____

Listening

5. As you listen to other students discuss their selections, what important points can you add about each selection? Add these details to the discussion.

_____

_____

_____

_____

_____

_____

Self-Reliance

Directions Write the answers to these questions. Use complete sentences.

Literary Terms

1. Think of a story or poem that you have read. Write the theme of the work and explain how you know it is the theme.

_____

_____

_____

_____

Reading on Your Own

2. As you read, use the Main Idea Graphic (Details). Record the main idea of each excerpt in each box on the graphic organizer. After reading, write the main idea or theme of the entire essay based on the ideas presented in each excerpt. Think of an example from your own life that supports the theme. Explain the example below.

_____

_____

_____

_____

Grammar Check

3. Identify the following sentences as either *declarative, exclamatory, imperative,* or *interrogative.*

Do you need to borrow a dollar?

_____

Please return the book to the library.

_____

That movie was so scary!

_____

I plan to visit Maria on Wednesday.

_____

Speaking

4. Imagine that you work for a major newspaper and have the chance to interview Emerson. Create a skit with a partner in which you ask Emerson how he feels about parts of today's society. For example, you may ask him how he feels about certain trends or fads in the school or community. Write your ideas below. Practice the skit with your partner and then perform for the class.

_____

_____

_____

_____

Listening

5. Listen as your classmates perform the interview skits. Evaluate Emerson's answers. Tell whether you think Emerson would have really responded the way he does in the skits.

_____

_____

_____

_____

Walden

Directions Write the answers to these questions. Use complete sentences.

Literary Terms

1. Write both a simile and a metaphor about Henry David Thoreau. Use the information presented about his life to create the figures of speech. Then tell why you chose the comparisons you did.

_____

_____

_____

_____

Reading on Your Own

2. After you finish reading the excerpt from *Walden*, choose two examples of figures of speech. Explain what effect each example has on the selection. What is Thoreau trying to show by using each figure of speech?

_____

_____

_____

_____

Grammar Check

3. Change the pronouns in the following sentences to first-person pronouns. Rewrite the sentences with the new pronouns below each original sentence.

She decided to go to the beach instead of the mall.

_____

They carried their surfboards down the hill.

_____

Janice taught him how to stand on the surfboard.

_____

Speaking

4. Choose a section of Thoreau's *Walden*. Read this section aloud many times until you feel comfortable with the text and can read with expression. Find a partner who chose a different section and read your section aloud to him or her. Below, write important words from your section that you want to emphasize when reading the text.

_____

_____

_____

Listening

5. Present your ideas for nature sound effects that may add to an audio or video recording of *Walden*. As you listen to other students present their ideas, which ideas do you like best? Which ideas do you think would add the most to the recording? Explain.

_____

_____

_____

_____

Dr. Heidegger's Experiment

Directions Write the answers to these questions. Use complete sentences.

Literary Terms

1. What is the difference between a theme and a moral? Can a story have both? Explain.

_____

_____

_____

_____

Reading on Your Own

2. As you read, find two examples of alliteration in the text. For each example, replace one or two of the alliterative words with a synonym. Which way is more effective—with alliteration or without? Explain.

_____

_____

_____

_____

_____

Grammar Check

3. Change the following sentences so that they use action verbs instead of state-of-being verbs.

He was in the Boston Marathon.

_____

_____

Tyra is always in a conversation with her friends during study hall.

_____

_____

Speaking

4. Imagine that the characters from "Dr. Heidegger's Experiment" are on a talk show to explain their experience with the water from the Fountain of Youth. Select classmates to play the roles of the five characters and a talk show host. In a group, create questions that the talk show host may ask and the characters' responses to those questions. Use the story to decide how characters may answer or act during the talk show. Practice the dialogue and then perform it in front of the class. On the lines below, write two strengths and two weaknesses of the performance.

_____

_____

_____

_____

Listening

5. After listening to an audio recording of another short story by Nathaniel Hawthorne, decide which story you like better. Explain your reasons below. Afterward, have a class discussion about which story your classmates like better. Listen carefully to students' opinions and their reasons. Respond to comments made by your classmates.

_____

_____

_____

_____

The Fiddler *and* Shiloh

Directions Write the answers to these questions. Use complete sentences.

Literary Terms

1. Besides "The Fiddler," what other stories have you read that are written in first-person point of view? What are the advantages of reading a story written in first-person point of view? What are the disadvantages? Explain using examples from one of the stories that you have read before.

_____

_____

_____

_____

_____

_____

Reading on Your Own

2. Dialogue, or the conversation among characters, is commonly used by authors as a method of characterization. It allows readers to understand the characters' personality traits and the relationships they have with each other. How does the dialogue in "The Fiddler" help you to understand the characters of Helmstone, Hautboy, and Standard?

_____

_____

_____

_____

Grammar Check

3. Rewrite the following sentences adding punctuation—commas, periods, or question marks—correctly.

"Do you want to go to the store" Chee asked

_____

"I think" he slowly began "that we should go to the deli for lunch"

_____

Speaking

4. Choose one of the following ways to read "Shiloh": sadly, excitedly, factually, with confusion. Practice reading the poem, emphasizing certain words or lines to create a certain tone. Also, experiment with different rates of speed and volume of your voice. Then read the poem for a small group of your classmates, using the emotion you practiced.

_____

_____

Listening

5. Listen to each group member's reading of "Shiloh." Which tone do you feel best matches the author's tone in the written poem? Explain.

_____

_____

_____

Poems by Emily Dickinson

Directions Write the answers to these questions. Use complete sentences.

Literary Terms

1. Give an example of a concrete symbol and an abstract symbol from any of the three poems. What is the difference between the two types of symbols?

_____

_____

_____

Reading on Your Own

2. After you finish reading each of the three poems, look over the summaries you have created for each stanza. For each poem, use the summaries to create a one-sentence summary of the whole poem.

_____

_____

_____

Grammar Check

3. Correct each sentence below, keeping in mind the rules of capitalization.

jamal went to the library to check out adventures of huckleberry finn.

_____

_____

jaime and will wanted to read another story by edgar allan poe, so they chose "the cask of amontillado."

_____

_____

Speaking

4. In the Speaking activity of your textbook, you listened to your classmates read one of Emily Dickinson's poems. Which readings were the most effective? What traits do the best readers have in common? Write your ideas below. Then discuss your ideas in a small group, clearly presenting your ideas and taking turns with others.

_____

_____

_____

_____

Listening

5. Listen to an audio recording of another Emily Dickinson poem. As you listen, write down those words that seem important to the poem. Afterward, look at the actual poem and compare your list to it. Are any words on your list capitalized in the poem? Do you feel these words should be emphasized in a reading of the poem? Explain.

_____

_____

_____

_____

Unit 2 Review

Directions Write the answers to these questions. Use complete sentences.

Literary Terms

1. Choose one of your favorite characters from the unit. Write two original similes about this character, keeping the mind the character traits or physical description presented in the text.

_____

_____

_____

_____

Reading on Your Own

2. After you read the Unit 2 summary, paraphrase, or put into your own words, the similarities that the authors and selections have in this unit.

_____

_____

_____

_____

_____

Grammar Check

Longer works such as plays, novels, and other books are punctuated by either underlining the title of the work or italicizing it. Collections of essays or poems are also underlined or italicized. However, shorter works such as poems and short stories are punctuated with quotation marks. Review the genre of each of the selections in this unit and then correctly punctuate the sentences in the next column.

3. We read Walden in class before we went to the park for a field trip.

_____

_____

_____

4. Hautboy from The Fiddler seems to believe in some of Ralph Waldo Emerson's ideas presented in Self-Reliance.

_____

_____

_____

_____

Speaking and Listening

5. Choose your favorite selection from this unit Why is it your favorite selection? What do you think the author does particularly well in his or her writing? Discuss in a small group your reasons for choosing the selection. Listen to other students' opinions and respond to their ideas. After discussing the selections in your group, has your opinion changed about any of the selections? Explain.

_____

_____

_____

_____

Spirituals

Directions Write the answers to these questions. Use complete sentences.

Literary Terms

1. What other genres of literature have you read that use dialect? Name one work that uses dialect and explain how it affected your understanding of the text.

_____

_____

_____

_____

Reading on Your Own

2. After reading the spirituals and identifying the repeated words and phrases, how do the refrains affect the tones of the spirituals? Are there other lines in the spirituals that you think would make good refrains? Explain.

_____

_____

_____

_____

_____

_____

Grammar Check

3. Below are three examples of words written in dialect. Write the correct spelling for each.

doin' _____

'em _____

gittin' _____

Speaking

4. Find another example of a spiritual on the Internet or at the school library. Compare and contrast the example to the other spirituals you have read. Write some of your observations below. Read your spiritual aloud to the class. Then share with the class some of the observations about the spiritual.

_____

_____

_____

_____

_____

_____

Listening

5. Create your own audio recording of one of the spirituals. Consider whether singing or reading it is more powerful. What words may you want to emphasize? How quickly should the spirituals be read or sung? What tone of voice should you use? Write down some of your ideas below. Share your audio recording with the class. As you listen to other recordings, which choices of your classmates do you think worked well? Which did not? Explain.

_____

_____

_____

_____

_____

_____

Thirty-Five

Directions Write the answers to these questions. Use complete sentences.

Literary Terms

1. Find a poem either on the Internet or in a book in the library. Identify the tone based on the poet's word choice, figurative language, punctuation, and subject matter of the work. Explain how you know it is the tone of the poem.

_____

_____

_____

_____

Reading on Your Own

2. Reread lines 29 through 34 in "Thirty-Five." How else could Sarah Josepha Hale have expressed this idea figuratively? Explain.

_____

_____

_____

_____

Grammar Check

3. Add either a period or an exclamation point to the end of each sentence. Below each sentence explain your reason for adding either a period or an exclamation point.

What fun I had today at school

_____

_____

I need to drink a glass of water

_____

_____

My third-period class is English

_____

_____

Speaking

4. Rewrite one stanza of the poem in prose form. Read the original stanza aloud to a partner, and then read the prose version aloud. How did the way you read the poem change from the original version to the prose version? Explain. Which way do you prefer?

_____

_____

_____

_____

_____

_____

Listening

5. As you listen to your teacher read the poem, what words are repeated throughout the poem? Record those words below. Why do you think Sarah Josepha Hale repeats these words? What effect does it have on the listener? Explain.

_____

_____

_____

_____

_____

_____

The Fugitive Blacksmith

Directions Write the answers to these questions. Use complete sentences.

Literary Terms

1. What are some of the different types of conflicts characters can have in a story? For each conflict, write an example from a story that you have read.

_____

_____

_____

Reading on Your Own

2. Think about why someone might want to read an autobiography. What does the reader gain by reading about someone else's experiences? Explain.

_____

_____

_____

_____

Grammar Check

3. For each of the following sentences, identify the adverbs and write them on the lines below.

I walked quickly to my silver car.

_____

_____

Jim patiently waited while his parents brought out his very large present.

_____

_____

Speaking

4. Imagine that James Pennington decided to stop in the city to tell his brother what he is doing. What might his brother say? How might James respond? Write your ideas below. Create a short skit and then perform it in front of the class. Try to capture James's character as shown throughout *The Fugitive Blacksmith*. Speak with emotions that James and his brother may be feeling at that moment.

_____

_____

_____

_____

_____

_____

_____

Listening

5. Listen as your teacher reads part of *The Fugitive Blacksmith* that comes before the selection in the book. What new understanding about James and his decision to run away do you get from listening to an earlier section of the autobiography? Explain.

_____

_____

_____

_____

Poems by Walt Whitman

Directions Write the answers to these questions. Use complete sentences.

Literary Terms

1. Which type of poem do you like better: a poem written in free verse or one with a structured rhyming pattern and line length? Explain.

_____

_____

_____

Reading on Your Own

2. Choose one of the stanzas in either of Whitman's poems that contains anaphora. Rewrite the stanza below so that it no longer contains anaphora. Read the new version. How does the poem affect the reader differently without the anaphora? Which way do you prefer? Explain.

_____

_____

_____

_____

_____

Grammar Check

3. For each of the following sentences, change either the statement into an interrogative sentence or the interrogative sentence into a statement.

They are going to the store.

_____

Should I study more for this test?

_____

Speaking

4. In a small group, discuss Whitman's purpose in writing "Beat! Beat! Drums!" What do you think Whitman wanted his readers to get from the poem? How does he show his point to his readers? Explain your ideas below before beginning the discussion.

_____

_____

_____

_____

_____

_____

Listening

5. In a group, practice reading aloud "Come Up from the Fields Father" in different ways. First, try just one person reading the whole poem. Next, try assigning parts such as the daughter's words or the mother's thoughts to different readers. Finally, try adding any sound effects your group feels may work in the poem. After each reading, identify how the changes affected you as a listener. Which way do you prefer? Explain.

_____

_____

_____

_____

A Letter to Mrs. Bixby

Directions Write the answers to these questions. Use complete sentences.

Literary Terms

1. Use a Sequence Chain graphic organizer to record the sequence of events of a recent story you have read. (You can get a copy of this organizer from your teacher.) Why is sequence so important in a story? Explain.

_____

_____

_____

Reading on Your Own

2. After reading President Lincoln's letter, how well did you predict the contents of the letter in Before Reading the Selection? Is there anything from your prediction that you felt Lincoln should have included in his letter but did not? Explain.

_____

_____

_____

_____

Grammar Check

3. When would you use a business letter versus a friendly letter? Identify specific times when you would use a business letter and times when you would use a friendly letter. Summarize some of the main differences between the two types of letters.

_____

_____

_____

_____

Speaking

4. Imagine that President Lincoln and Mrs. Bixby were good friends. Rewrite the letter so that it reflects a friendly letter style rather than a business letter. Read your letter aloud to a partner. How has the tone of the letter changed? How has the content changed? Which letter do you think would offer Mrs. Bixby more comfort? Explain.

_____

_____

_____

_____

_____

_____

Listening

5. In a small group, practice reading "A Letter to Mrs. Bixby" aloud. How might Lincoln have wanted to sound? Formal? Caring? Listen to each group member's reading of the letter as they try to capture Lincoln's voice. Which reading do you think best represents the way Lincoln wanted to sound? Explain.

_____

_____

_____

_____

_____

_____

What the Black Man Wants

Directions Write the answers to these questions. Use complete sentences.

Literary Terms

1. In society today, what are some of the symbols used to represent the following ideas: freedom, independence, justice? Why are these symbols so important to our society?

_____

_____

_____

_____

Reading on Your Own

2. After reading the story, how well did you predict what the speech would be about? What parts of the speech surprised you? What parts did you correctly predict? Explain. After reading the speech, what other title could the speech have?

_____

_____

_____

_____

Grammar Check

3. Underline the prepositions in the following sentences. Circle the objects of the prepositions.

- On Wednesday, I swam for an hour in the cold water.

- I enjoy walking in the mall and talking to my friends.

- I bought her gift during the big sale at the store.

Speaking

4. Why do you think Frederick Douglass was considered such an effective writer and speaker? Write your thoughts below and then have a class discussion. Be sure to use specific examples from the text when you offer your opinions in the class discussion.

_____

_____

_____

_____

_____

_____

Listening

5. As you listen to your teacher read aloud the selection, which areas of the speech do you feel Douglass does a good job of providing details and examples to support his points? Where do you feel it would be helpful for him to add more supporting details or examples? What other examples might he add? Explain.

_____

_____

_____

_____

_____

_____

Life on the Mississippi

Directions Write the answers to these questions. Use complete sentences.

Literary Terms

1. Use imagery to describe the cafeteria at your school in three sentences. Be sure to use words that appeal to all five senses.

_____

_____

_____

_____

Reading on Your Own

2. As you read *Life on the Mississippi,* how do you think you would react as the steamboat comes into town? Do you think that your dream would also be to become a steamboat pilot if you lived in the town? Explain.

_____

_____

_____

Grammar Check

3. On a separate sheet of paper, rewrite the paragraph below. Add transitions to help show the relationships between the ideas.

Jim and I had a long day running errands. We went to the bank to deposit our checks. We went to the mall to return my red sweater for a blue one. At the mall, we ate pizza for lunch. We stopped by the grocery store to pick up some steaks for dinner. We stopped to put gas in the car on our way home.

Speaking

4. Imagine that Mark Twain runs into the one boy who goes away and then turns up as an apprentice engineer. Create a short conversation between the two of them. What might the boy say? How might Twain respond? Write your ideas below. Consider the way Twain feels about the boy and his description of the boy in the text. Practice the skit with a partner and perform it in front of the class. Use body language to show the way both boys feel during the conversation.

_____

_____

_____

_____

Listening

5. Imagine that you are on the steamboat as it comes into the town. What would your opinion of the town be as an outsider looking in? What sights and sounds of the town would you notice? Explain your ideas below. Then listen as your classmates explain their opinions and observations. How many students have ideas similar to yours? What are some opinions that are very different from your own? Write these below.

_____

_____

_____

_____

The Old Chisholm Trail

Directions Write the answers to these questions. Use complete sentences.

Literary Terms

1. Write a short stanza about your favorite movie using end rhyme. Be sure the last words of two lines rhyme with one another.

_____

_____

_____

_____

Reading on Your Own

2. What do you do when you are working and want to pass the time? Do you listen to music or sing to yourself? How are the ways you pass the time similar to the spirituals or ballads used by the African slaves or the cowhands? How are they different? Explain.

_____

_____

_____

_____

Grammar Check

3. On the line below each sentence, write the verb. Then identify the tense—past, present, or future—of the verb.

He ran into the goalie while trying to score the goal.

_____

She runs for at least 30 minutes each day.

_____

I will run after school to get in shape.

_____

Speaking

4. After researching the history of cattle drives and the difficulties of moving cattle, what qualities must a person have to be a successful cowhand? Create a speech in which you identify those qualities a good cowhand must have. Support your opinion with supporting details and facts from your research. Create a brief outline of your speech below.

_____

_____

_____

_____

_____

Listening

5. Practice reading "The Old Chisholm Trail" aloud. Create new lines for the chorus that still capture the feeling in the ballad and write them below. Read the ballad to a small group, adding your new lines after each stanza instead of the original chorus. As you listen to others read their new lines in the ballad, which new lines do you think best capture the main idea of the original ballad? Explain.

_____

_____

_____

_____

This Sacred Soil

Directions Write the answers to these questions. Use complete sentences.

Literary Terms

1. Create a sentence using alliteration. To get started, consider sounds that are related to certain things. For example, a snake is often identified with the "s" sound, creating a feeling of sneakiness or evil. Then, think about words that could describe the appearance or movement of certain things.

_____

_____

_____

_____

Reading on Your Own

2. Use a Main Idea Graphic organizer to record Chief Seattle's main idea and supporting details as you read his speech. (You can get a copy of this organizer from your teacher.) How do the ideas in the graphic organizer compare or contrast to your predictions from Before Reading the Selection? Explain.

_____

_____

_____

_____

Grammar Check

3. For each of the following sentences, add commas correctly to the series of words or phrases.

- Bowling swimming and running are my favorite activities to do during summer break.

- I hope to finish my math science and social studies homework in study hall today.

- On Friday night we went to the movies ate pizza at the pizza shop and played games at the arcade.

Speaking

4. Imagine that you are Isaac Stevens as you read "This Sacred Soil." Create a short conversation between Isaac Stevens and Chief Seattle after he gives his speech. What might Isaac Stevens say to Chief Seattle? How might Chief Seattle respond? Write your ideas below. Practice your skit with a partner and then perform it in front of the class.

_____

_____

_____

_____

Listening

5. As you listen to another American speech, notice the similarities of the two speeches. What are the differences between the two speeches? What do these speeches show you about the attitudes of the Americans? Explain.

_____

_____

_____

_____

Zuni and Makah Lullabies

Directions Write the answers to these questions. Use complete sentences.

Literary Terms

1. Create your own four-line lullaby. Remember that a lullaby is a soothing song or poem sung to a baby.

_____

_____

_____

_____

Reading on Your Own

2. Besides animals, what other objects or ideas might appear in an American Indian lullaby based on what you know of the culture? Explain.

_____

_____

_____

Grammar Check

3. Choose a lullaby that you heard or sang as a child. Rewrite the lullaby or part of the lullaby below, using your best handwriting. Be sure to use the correct capitalization and punctuation as you rewrite the lullaby.

_____

_____

_____

_____

_____

Speaking

4. After researching the importance of language to infants, create a one-day schedule for a baby. Include activities that will help that baby develop language. In a small group, discuss your schedules. What similar activities do the schedules have? Does someone have an activity that you would like to add to your schedule? Explain.

_____

_____

_____

_____

Listening

5. Locate music that might be played as background music for the Zuni and Makah lullabies. Listen to several songs and types of music. Choose a song for each of the lullabies. How do the songs help to develop the feelings and tone of the different lullabies? Explain.

_____

_____

_____

_____

I Will Fight No More Forever

Directions Write the answers to these questions. Use complete sentences.

Literary Terms

1. Write a short paragraph in which you use repetition to create a certain effect. For example, Chief Joseph uses the words *dead*, *freezing*, and *tired* many times to emphasize how he and his people are feeling.

_____
_____
_____
_____
_____

Reading on Your Own

2. Use a Main Idea Graphic (Details) organizer to record Chief Joseph's reasons for surrendering. (You can get a copy of this organizer from your teacher.) Then decide if you think Chief Joseph is a good or bad leader. Explain your opinion using support from the speech.

_____
_____
_____

Grammar Check

3. Rewrite the following sentences. If contractions are used, rewrite the sentences without contractions. If contractions are not used, rewrite the sentence using contractions.

They are not supposed to be in the hallway during class time.

_____
_____

I can't imagine what he said to make her so angry.

_____
_____

I am angry because he will not go to the store with me.

_____
_____

Speaking

4. Rewrite Chief Joseph's speech, replacing the words he repeats with synonyms. Write the synonyms below. Practice reading the new speech aloud. Be sure to emphasize important words and show the feelings Chief Joseph might have had. Read your speech to a small group.

_____
_____
_____

Listening

5. As you listen to your classmates read their new speeches from the Speaking activity, do you think the original speech or the new speech is more effective as it is read to the audience? Explain. Which synonyms do you think best replace the words in Chief Joseph's original speech? Explain.

_____
_____
_____

Unit 3 Review

Directions Write the answers to these questions. Use complete sentences.

Literary Terms

1. As an author, what are some of the advantages to using dialect in a piece of writing? What might be some of the disadvantages to using dialect? Explain.

_____

_____

_____

_____

Reading on Your Own

2. As you read the summaries of the different selections in this unit, which authors come from similar backgrounds and experiences? Choose two authors and compare the experiences that they have had. Use details from the different texts to support your point.

_____

_____

_____

_____

_____

Grammar Check

As you read the Unit 3 Summary, notice that some selection titles are in quotation marks. Others are italicized (or underlined). Use the examples in the summary to determine how each of the following genres are punctuated. Write the correct answer on each line.

3. poetry _____

song _____

4. autobiography _____

speech _____

Speaking and Listening

5. After reading the Unit 3 Summary, choose your favorite selection from this unit. Create a speech explaining why it is your favorite selection. Consider literary elements, content, and purpose as reasons for your choice. Practice your speech, using transitions between each point to support your opinion. Present your speech to a small group. As you listen to others give their speeches, do you agree or disagree with their opinions of a selection? Explain the reasons why you agree or disagree below.

_____

_____

_____

_____

The Open Boat

Directions Write the answers to these questions. Use complete sentences.

Literary Terms

1. Think about a book or story you have recently read. Use the Plot Mountain graphic organizer to identify the rising action, climax, and resolution of the story. How do you know what the climax of the story is? Explain.

_____

_____

_____

_____

Reading on Your Own

2. After you finish reading "The Open Boat," evaluate your prediction of the end of the story. How well did you predict the ending? What surprised you about the ending? Do you think Stephen Crane should have ended the story another way? Explain.

_____

_____

_____

Grammar Check

3. Rewrite the following dialogue using quotation marks, punctuation, and paragraphs correctly.

Did you read Stephen Crane's "The Open Boat" she asked. Oh yes I replied. Then she said his characters are often victims of a cold and grim fate.

_____

_____

_____

_____

_____

_____

Speaking

4. Imagine you are going to interview the surviving characters about their experience and the oiler's death. Write your questions below. Then ask your classmates to play the part of the characters and respond your questions.

_____

_____

_____

Listening

5. Find another poem that you think deals with the feelings and themes in "The Open Boat." Read your poem to the class. As you listen to others read their poems, what connections can you make between their poem and the short story. Write your observations below.

_____

_____

_____

To Build a Fire

Directions Write the answers to these questions. Use complete sentences.

Literary Terms

1. Think about the meaning of *foreshadowing*. How does foreshadowing keep readers interested in the story? Explain.

_____

_____

_____

_____

Reading on Your Own

2. As you read, consider the man's character. He ignores the warnings of those older than him. Think of this story in a different setting. Write the setting below. Then explain how even in a different setting the man may still end up with the same fate.

_____

_____

_____

_____

Speaking and Listening

5. Think about this question: How responsible do you feel the man is for his own death? Rate your feelings on a scale of 1–10. A 1 means the death is not his fault at all and a 10 means it is totally his fault. Write that number below. Then discuss your opinion with a small group. During the discussion, speak clearly so that others are able to hear you. Listen carefully to others discuss their opinions. How are your ratings different? Explain.

_____

_____

_____

_____

_____

_____

Grammar Check

Jim and Alice decided to go to the movies.

3. Write the subject of the sentence above.

_____

_____

4. Write the predicate of the sentence above. Underline the verb.

_____

_____

Unit 4 Review

Directions Write the answers to these questions. Use complete sentences.

Literary Terms

1. Change the following sentence so that it uses personification and is more interesting for the reader: *The leaves blew across the yard as the storm approached.*

_____

_____

_____

Reading on Your Own

2. As you read the Unit 4 summary, identify the similarities and differences between naturalism and realism. Write your observations below.

_____

_____

_____

_____

Grammar Check

A subject complement is a word that describes or renames the subject of a sentence. Subject complements can be either nouns or adjectives. Subject complements that are nouns are called *predicate nominatives.* Subject complements that are adjectives are called *predicate adjectives.* For example, *She is a teacher.* In this sentence, *teacher* is the subject complement. It is a predicate nominative because *teacher* is a noun that renames the subject of the sentence, *she.* In the sentence *She is funny,* the word *funny* is a predicate adjective because it describes *she.*

For each of the following sentences, circle the subject complement. Then write whether it is a predicate nominative (PN) or predicate adjective (PA) below.

3. Working in factories was difficult.

_____

4. Politicians of the time were liars.

_____

Speaking and Listening

5. Which short story do you like better, "The Open Boat" or "To Build a Fire"? Explain your reasons below using details from the story. Then discuss your opinion with a partner. Listen carefully to your partner's choice. How are your choices similar or different?

_____

_____

_____

_____

_____

_____

Trifles

Directions Write the answers to these questions. Use complete sentences.

Literary Terms

1. How is reading a drama similar to reading a short story? How is it different?

_____

_____

_____

_____

Reading on Your Own

2. Recall the prediction you made about the play before you began reading. Was your prediction similar to what actually happened? How was it different?

_____

_____

_____

_____

_____

Grammar Check

3. Rewrite the following sentences using correct grammar.

I knew they must be up, it was past eight o'clock.

_____

_____

How do, Mrs. Wright, it's cold, ain't it?

_____

_____

Speaking

4. What do you think will happen when the Sheriff and the County Attorney return to the jail and talk to Mrs. Wright? Write your answer below. Then, on another sheet of paper, create a skit about the Sheriff and the County Attorney's conversation with Mrs. Wright. Be sure to include stage directions. Practice your skit with other classmates and then perform it in front of the class.

_____

_____

_____

_____

_____

Listening

5. Listen to your classmates present their skits. Which group do you think does the best job of capturing the Sheriff's and County Attorney's personalities? Which group does the best job of capturing the feelings of the characters? Explain.

_____

_____

_____

_____

_____

The Far and the Near

Directions Write the answers to these questions. Use complete sentences.

Literary Terms

1. Think of a book or movie that you have recently seen. Identify the protagonist and antagonist in the book or movie. Then tell how the conflict was resolved. Write your observations below.

_____

_____

_____

_____

_____

Reading on Your Own

2. As you read, record important words that the narrator uses to describe the woman, her child, and their home. How do these words help to create a change in tone as the story progresses?

_____

_____

_____

_____

Grammar Check

3. Circle the conjunctions in the following sentence.

Bill and Jack wanted to water ski and swim, but they did not have time to do both.

Speaking

4. What do you think the mother and daughter said to each other after the engineer left? Write your ideas below. Then, on another sheet of paper, create a conversation between the mother and daughter. Practice your skit, using actions, gestures, and speech to show how you believe each character might have looked and acted. Keep in mind how the author describes each character in the story.

_____

_____

_____

_____

_____

Listening

5. Think of your worst day at school and tell a partner the story. As you listen to your partner tell his or her story, write down the details that cause you to feel sympathy for your partner. Also write the details that cause you to feel empathy for him or her.

_____

_____

_____

_____

Theme for English B

Directions Write the answers to these questions. Use complete sentences.

Literary Terms

1. What do you think are the advantages of writing in free verse? What are some of the disadvantages? Explain.

_____

_____

_____

_____

_____

Reading on Your Own

2. Langston Hughes was an African American living in the first half of the 1900s. What ideas did you predict to be a part of his poem? What ideas in his poem surprised you?

_____

_____

_____

_____

Grammar Check

3. Rewrite the following sentence. Add dashes to show a pause or break in thought.

You see this may not work out the way we thought it would or could.

_____

_____

_____

_____

Speaking

4. Do you think Langston Hughes' poem still relates to today's society? Explain your opinion below. Then discuss your opinion with a partner, using examples to support your opinion.

_____

_____

_____

_____

_____

_____

Listening

5. How do you imagine Langston Hughes's tone as he reads this poem? Write your opinion below. Then practice reading aloud Hughes's poem using that tone. Afterward, listen to other students read the poem. What tones have they chosen? Which do you feel best fits Hughes's message? Explain.

_____

_____

_____

_____

_____

_____

The Sculptor's Funeral

Directions Write the answers to these questions. Use complete sentences.

Literary Terms

1. Circle the letter of the answer that is not a way authors often develop characters.

    A the character's physical description

    B the character's actions

    C other characters' comments about the character

    D other characters' decisions

Reading on Your Own

2. Choose one of the characters in the story. As you read, complete a Character Analysis Guide graphic organizer. Decide the character traits of that character and the way the author creates these traits. What do you see as the main trait of your character?

_____

_____

_____

_____

Grammar Check

Rewrite the following sentences. Add semicolons where they are necessary.

3. He does not need lunch money he packed his lunch today.

_____

_____

_____

4. Maria wanted to change the carpet in the living room, dining room, and bedroom, the lights in the bathroom, and the tile in the kitchen.

_____

_____

_____

_____

Speaking and Listening

5. Choose a partner. One person should represent a townsperson other than Jim Laird. The other should be Harvey Merrick. Decide whether your character would agree or disagree with the quote, "Home is where the heart is." Write your opinion below. Then write a speech in which your character defends why the quote is true or untrue. Present your speech to your partner. As you listen to your partner's speech, what similarities and differences exist between the two speeches?

_____

_____

_____

_____

_____

_____

_____

The Freshest Boy

Directions Write the answers to these questions. Use complete sentences.

Literary Terms

1. What are the similarities between an autobiography and a semiautobiography? What are the differences? Explain.

_____

_____

_____

_____

_____

Reading on Your Own

2. Decide how well you predicted what the story would be about from the title. Do you think "The Freshest Boy" is an appropriate title? What other title do you think would work well with this story? Explain.

_____

_____

_____

_____

Grammar Check

3. Rewrite the following sentence. Use correct capitalization, spelling, and punctuation.

I'm going to see romeo and juliet because it is my favorete play

_____

_____

_____

Speaking

4. Do you think the way Fitzgerald presents teenage behavior is correct? Would the story be different if Fitzgerald had used female characters? Write your opinion below. Then form a small group with your classmates and discuss your opinions.

_____

_____

_____

_____

_____

_____

_____

Listening

5. Try eavesdropping on a conversation taking place in your school. What can be some of the negative things about eavesdropping on a conversation? Are there positive parts about eavesdropping? Explain.

_____

_____

_____

_____

_____

_____

_____

Poems by Robert Frost

Directions Write the answers to these questions. Use complete sentences.

Literary Terms

1. Why might an author decide to use rhyme scheme instead of free verse? Explain.

_____

_____

_____

_____

Reading on Your Own

2. Compare and contrast the moods of the three Frost poems. Which two poems are most similar? Is there one that stands out as very different from the others? Explain.

_____

_____

_____

_____

Grammar Check

3. Change the following sentence from Frost's "Fire and Ice" so that it has a more common syntax.

"I think I know enough of hate to say that for destruction ice is also great and would suffice."

_____

_____

_____

_____

Speaking

4. Practice reading aloud lines 1–19 or lines 20–45 in "Mending Wall." Think about how you might show the mood of the poem as you read it aloud. Decide what words you will stress in the poem. Use the punctuation marks to figure out where to pause and how to pace your reading. Write some of your ideas below. Afterward, record your reading. Play your recording for a small group.

_____

_____

_____

_____

_____

_____

Listening

5. As you listen to your classmates' recordings of "Mending Wall," decide what the line "Something there is that doesn't love a wall" means. Does listening to the poem aloud help you to understand better the meaning of this line? Explain.

_____

_____

_____

_____

_____

Poems by Carl Sandburg

Directions Write the answers to these questions. Use complete sentences.

Literary Terms

1. Write two sentences using alliteration and onomatopoeia.

_____

_____

_____

_____

Reading on Your Own

2. Circle the letter of the image that contrasts the image of two people fighting in "Jazz Fantasia."

A green lanterns calling to the high soft stars

B autumn wind moaning in the lonesome treetops

C race car slipping away from a motorcycle cop

D two people tumbling down the stairs

Grammar Check

3. Choose one of the other poems from this unit such as "A Time to Talk" or "Fire and Ice." On another sheet of paper rewrite the poem adding ellipses in places that you think are appropriate. Look at Sandburg's poems to see how he uses ellipses to create an effect. Write your reasons for adding ellipses to the poem.

_____

_____

_____

Speaking

4. Use resources in your school library and find a free verse poem that uses alliteration, onomatopoeia, or repetition. Practice reading the poem aloud several times. Then decide which words you need to give importance to. Also note the areas where you need to speed up or slow down your reading. Write those decisions below. Read the poem aloud to your class.

_____

_____

_____

_____

_____

Listening

5. Listen to your classmates read their poems aloud. Write down any onomatopoeic words you hear. Then explain how onomatopoeia affects the poetry?

_____

_____

_____

_____

_____

Poems by William Carlos Williams

Directions Write the answers to these questions. Use complete sentences.

Literary Terms

1. Write 2–3 sentences that create a sensory image. Use words and phrases that refer to the five senses.

_____

_____

_____

_____

_____

Reading on Your Own

2. As you read each poem, draw a picture of the image that comes to your mind. Compare and contrast your pictures with a partner's pictures. What similarities do you notice in each of the pictures?

_____

_____

_____

Grammar Check

3. Write the poem "This Is Just To Say" out as a paragraph. Write in complete sentences. Use correct capitalization and punctuation such as commas and periods.

_____

_____

_____

_____

Speaking

4. Find another poem by William Carlos Williams either at the school library or on the Internet. Practice reading the poem aloud. As you read, concentrate on your speaking skills and nonverbal language. What tone will you use? On the lines below, write the tone. Also tell how you will try to show this tone using your voice and body language.

_____

_____

_____

_____

_____

_____

Listening

5. Listen as your classmates read other poems by William Carlos Williams. What similarities do you notice between these poems and the two poems in this selection?

_____

_____

_____

_____

_____

_____

Unit 5 Review

Directions Write the answers to these questions. Use complete sentences.

Literary Terms

1. Circle which of the following is not an example of a setting from this unit.

   A a dark, stormy city

   B a boy's school

   C a cold, messy farmhouse

   D a hotel in the city

Reading on Your Own

2. As you read the Unit 5 Summary, carefully consider all of the important events during the time period. Summarize the time period below in one or two sentences.

   _____

   _____

   _____

Grammar Check

A simple sentence is a sentence with only one independent clause. For example, *The dog went outside.* A compound sentence has two or more independent clauses. For example, *The dog went outside, and he slept in the sun.* Decide whether each of the following sentences is simple (S) or compound (C). Write either *S* or *C* on each line. If the sentence is compound, put parentheses around each independent clause.

3. I wanted to go to the park, but I had to do my homework. _____

4. We stayed home on Saturday night to get some rest. _____

Speaking and Listening

5. Choose your favorite poem from the unit. On the lines below, write why it is your favorite. Then share your reasons with the class. For example, do you like the rhyme scheme? Do you like it because it is a free verse poem? Listen carefully to your classmates describe their favorite poems.

   _____

   _____

   _____

   _____

   _____

   _____

   _____

   _____

   _____

To Be Young, Gifted and Black

Directions Write the answers to these questions. Use complete sentences.

Literary Terms

1. Compare and contrast an autobiography and biography. How are they similar? How are they different?

_____

_____

_____

_____

Reading on Your Own

2. Using a Venn Diagram, described in Appendix A, record memories of your childhood in one of the circles. Record memories of Lorraine Hansberry's childhood in the other circle. Where the circles overlap, record those parts of your childhood that are the same as Hansberry's. Write one similarity and one difference between the two childhoods below.

_____

_____

_____

_____

Grammar Check

3. Change the following sentence from passive voice to active voice: *The red sweater was worn by the young girl.*

_____

_____

_____

Speaking and Listening

4. After completing research on birth order, arrange to interview someone with that birth order about his or her experience. To prepare for the interview, write your questions below. During the interview, be sure to listen carefully and take notes on another sheet of paper. Afterward, compare the answers to your research. Have a class discussion about how well your interview supports your research.

_____

_____

_____

_____

_____

_____

_____

_____

_____

_____

_____

_____

The Killers

Directions Write the answers to these questions. Use complete sentences.

Literary Terms

1. Circle the statement that is **not** a comment describing an author's style.

   A The author often uses similes when he writes.

   B The author uses short, direct sentences.

   C The climax of the story is when the men decide whether to stay or go.

   D The characters are mostly developed through dialogue.

Reading on Your Own

2. Choose one of the characters in the story. Complete a Character Analysis Guide, described in Appendix A, for this character. Below, write the character trait that is most developed in the story. Give at least two examples from the text to support this trait.

_____

_____

_____

_____

_____

Grammar Check

3. Rewrite the following sentence adding commas where necessary.

Tim wanted a peanut butter and jelly sandwich an apple and a glass of milk for lunch.

_____

_____

_____

Speaking

4. What do you think will happen to Ole Andreson? Write your ideas below. On another sheet of paper, create a skit to show what happens when Ole Andreson meets the killers. Use dialogue as the main way to develop the plot as Hemingway does. Practice your skit and then perform it in front of the class.

_____

_____

_____

_____

_____

_____

_____

_____

Listening

5. As you listen to others perform their skits, what sound effects do you think would help make the situation feel real if it were to be broadcast over radio? Write your ideas below.

_____

_____

_____

_____

_____

_____

_____

Flight

Directions Write the answers to these questions. Use complete sentences.

Literary Terms

1. Steinbeck uses animal imagery to describe the characters in "Flight." Mama calls Pepé a "big sheep," "big coyote," and "foolish chicken." All of these terms help the reader understand Pepé's character. If you were to write a story about one of your friends or family members, what animal imagery would you use so that your reader would understand what that person is like? Below, write the name of your friend or family member. Then choose an animal that you think best represents the personality traits of that person. Give three supporting details as to why that animal is a good choice to understand your chosen person's character.

_____

_____

_____

_____

_____

_____

Reading on Your Own

2. Write how your prediction of the story's ending differs from the actual story ending. What clues did you use in the opening pages of the story to make your prediction?

_____

_____

_____

Grammar Check

3. Add commas to the following sentence where they are necessary: *Jill remember to turn off the light.*

Speaking

4. Imagine you are on the local school board. The board is trying to decide on an appropriate punishment for those students who are truant. What do you think is the proper punishment? Write your ideas below. Then, on another sheet of paper, create a dialogue of a school board meeting on this topic. Be sure to include the opinions of parents or students who may also be attending the meeting. Present your dialogue to the class.

_____

_____

_____

Listening

5. As you listen to the skits of the school board meeting, read along with a copy of the script. How well do the performers follow the emotions of the lines? Write your suggestions for improving the performance below.

_____

_____

_____

In Honor of David Anderson Brooks, My Father

Directions Write the answers to these questions. Use complete sentences.

Literary Terms

1. Why do you think the poet chose to include a subtitle? Would another subtitle be more appropriate? Explain.

_____

_____

_____

_____

Reading on Your Own

2. Choose one stanza of the poem that you think is the most difficult to understand. Rewrite the stanza below in prose form. What new understanding do you have after reading it in prose form?

_____

_____

_____

_____

_____

Grammar Check

3. Rewrite the following sentence. Change all of the singular nouns to plural nouns.

The ranch near the town has a well where a person throws a penny for good luck.

_____

_____

_____

Speaking

4. After reading Before Reading the Selection, what do you admire about Gwendolyn Brooks? Write your ideas below. Then, on another sheet of paper, write a requiem in which you honor some aspect of the poet's life. Remember that in a requiem there is an emotional connection between the poet and the subject of the poem. Give your poem a rhyme scheme. Read your poem aloud to a partner.

_____

_____

_____

_____

_____

_____

Listening

5. As you listen to your partner's requiem, what rhyme scheme does it have? Does the poem have a steady beat? If the poem were to be turned into a song, what instruments do you think would be used? Would the song be fast or slow?

_____

_____

_____

_____

_____

_____

The Catbird Seat

Directions Write the answers to these questions. Use complete sentences.

Literary Terms

1. In the story, Mrs. Barrows uses a number of idioms. Ask friends or relatives for examples of common idioms used today. Try to find at least two idioms. Write the idioms below and explain what they mean.

_____

_____

_____

_____

_____

Reading on Your Own

2. Recall the satire you read in Unit 1, "Wouter Van Twiller." Which satire do you think creates more humor? Which one did you enjoy more? Explain.

_____

_____

_____

_____

Grammar Check

3. Circle the letter of the sentence that does not have subject and verb agreement.

A Neither Jane nor Jim was ready for the big test.

B Each boy thought his experiment was the best.

C Kate is the fastest ninth grader on the girls' track team.

D Everybody were upset with the decision to cancel the show.

Speaking

4. What do you think will happen to Mrs. Barrows after the story ends? Write your opinion below. Afterward, discuss your opinion in a small group. Be sure to speak clearly and confidently. List details from the text to support your opinion, and take turns with others when speaking.

_____

_____

_____

_____

_____

_____

Listening

5. As other students present their ideas on what happens to Mrs. Barrows, listen carefully and attentively to their ideas. Which ideas do you feel are most possible based on Mrs. Barrows' personality in the text? Which ideas do you feel are least possible? Explain.

_____

_____

_____

_____

_____

_____

_____

Hiroshima

Directions Write the answers to these questions. Use complete sentences.

Literary Terms

1. What events in history in the past 10 years do you feel would make good topics for nonfiction books? Explain.

_____

_____

_____

_____

_____

_____

_____

_____

_____

_____

_____

_____

Reading on Your Own

2. Before you read *Hiroshima*, how did you feel about America's decision to drop the atomic bomb on Hiroshima and Nagasaki? After reading the excerpt, did your opinion change? Explain.

_____

_____

_____

_____

_____

Grammar Check

3. Rewrite the following long sentence, breaking it up into two or three smaller sentences. "Wanting to go to the movies, Jill, who had not done her chores yet, first cleaned up her room, then did the dishes overflowing in the sink, and finally swept the kitchen floor with a broom before approaching her parents, who had threatened to ground her earlier that day, for permission."

Speaking

4. Get a copy of Chapter 1 of Hersey's *Hiroshima*. Practice reading a section of the chapter aloud. Speak clearly so that the audience can understand what you are saying. Make sure you can pronounce each word in the section. What speaking skills do you want to focus on as you read? Write your goals below. Then read your selection to a partner, and ask for feedback on your speaking skills.

_____

_____

_____

Listening

5. As you listen to your partner read Chapter 1 of *Hiroshima*, how does this chapter help prepare readers for Chapter 2? What important plot details does the writer introduce? Explain.

_____

_____

_____

Notes of a Native Son

Directions Write the answers to these questions. Use complete sentences.

Literary Terms

1. Explain the relationship between tone and voice in a work. Are they the same thing? Does one help the other? Explain.

_____

_____

_____

_____

Reading on Your Own

2. After reading the excerpt from Baldwin's essay, which of Baldwin's comments do you identify with and understand? Which sentences speak to you? Explain.

_____

_____

_____

Grammar Check

For each sentence, add either dashes or parentheses to set off extra information. Rewrite each sentence below.

3. Jim wanted to take me to the movies probably an action movie after dinner.

_____

_____

4. She had many positive qualities generosity, dedication, and humor but she could not see them.

_____

_____

Speaking and Listening

5. Baldwin says in one of his last lines: ". . . I have many responsibilities, but none greater than this: to last, as Hemingway says . . ." What does Baldwin mean by this? Consider what you know about Hemingway from this unit. Is this idea present in his life and work? Write your ideas below and then discuss them as a class. As you listen to other students present their ideas, what are some of the different ways students interpret the word "last"? What similarities and differences do you find between your ideas and other students' ideas?

_____

_____

_____

_____

_____

_____

_____

_____

Stride Toward Freedom: The Montgomery Story

Directions Write the answers to these questions. Use complete sentences.

Literary Terms

1. Think of a song that uses repetition. What effect does this repetition have on the listener's overall understanding of the song? Explain.

_____

_____

Reading on Your Own

2. Use the Structured Overview graphic organizer, described in Appendix A, to record Martin Luther King Jr.'s different ideas for ways to deal with oppression. In the top box, write "ways to deal with oppression." Fill in the rest of the organizer using information from the selection. After filling out the organizer, do you agree with King's suggestion as to which path people should follow? Explain.

_____

_____

_____

_____

Grammar Check

3. Circle the transitions in the following short paragraph.

We decided that we wanted to start a chess club at the school. First, we had to find a teacher that would sponsor the club. In the meantime, we also got the necessary paperwork from the school principal. Next, we had to find people who would be interested in joining the club. After all of this work, we were ready for our first meeting. Finally, we could begin playing chess!

Speaking

4. Imagine that you have been asked to interview Martin Luther King Jr.'s son, Martin Luther King III, about how well he feels his father would react to society today. Write four questions and then interview a partner who pretends to be King's son.

_____

_____

_____

_____

_____

_____

Listening

5. Watch a video of another famous speaker such as John F. Kennedy or a politician such as President George W. Bush. Compare and contrast the speaker with Martin Luther King Jr. Pay attention to voice and body language. Which speaker do you think is more effective? Explain.

_____

_____

_____

_____

Monet's Waterlilies

Directions Write the answers to these questions. Use complete sentences.

Literary Terms

1. A paradox is a statement that includes opposite meanings but still makes sense. Find an example of a paradox in the selection and explain its meaning below.

_____

_____

_____

Reading on Your Own

2. Fill out a KWL Chart, described in Appendix A, about events that happened in Selma, Alabama, and Saigon, Vietnam. What do you know about these places? What do you want to know? Do research to answer your questions. In the third column, write what you have learned from your research. How does this new knowledge affect your understanding of the poem?

_____

_____

_____

Grammar Check

3. The following sentence is written in present tense: *Jim eats dinner with his mother and father once a week.* Rewrite the sentence in both future tense and past tense.

Future tense: _____

_____

Past tense: _____

_____

Speaking

4. Find a famous painting that interests you in some way. Study the painting, noticing small details, brush strokes, and color. What does it make you think about? Write some of your observations below. Afterward, on another sheet of paper, write a poem about your reaction to the painting. Practice reading your poem aloud until you can read it fluently and with expression.

_____

_____

_____

_____

Listening

5. As you watch and listen to the television news reports from the time period of the Vietnam War and civil rights movement, what similarities do you notice between that time period and the present? Create a Venn Diagram, described in Appendix A, to show the similarities and differences. Write what you think is the greatest difference and the greatest similarity between the two time periods.

_____

_____

_____

_____

Unit 6 Review

Directions Write the answers to these questions. Use complete sentences.

Literary Terms

1. Think of a recent story or book that you have read. What is the mood of the selection? How does the writer create it? Write the title of the selection and the mood below. Then explain how the author creates it.

_____

_____

_____

_____

Reading on Your Own

2. After you read the Unit 6 summary, write one or two sentences that summarize the time period covered in this unit.

_____

_____

_____

_____

Grammar Check

When writing dialogue, the end punctuation that goes with the dialogue is inside the quotation marks. However, the punctuation following an introductory statement such as "he said" or "she commented" goes outside of the quotation marks. Rewrite the following dialogues, using the correct punctuation.

3. Martha said I'm not going to school today because I'm sick

_____

_____

4. I really want to go she continued but how can I concentrate when I don't feel well

_____

_____

Speaking and Listening

5. Choose one of the selections from this unit. Write down the important ideas or plot events presented in the selection. Include important details about the author's or poet's life. In addition, decide the genre of the selection. Get together in a group with students who have chosen other selections. Present your information to them. As you listen to others present their information, write down the important points on another sheet of paper and decide if the students have forgotten anything that should be included. Be sure the students identify the correct genre of literature for each selection.

_____

_____

_____

_____

_____

_____

_____

_____

A Simile

Directions Write the answers to these questions. Use complete sentences.

Literary Terms

1. Write two similes that would help to create a lighthearted mood in a poem.

_____

_____

_____

_____

Reading on Your Own

2. Rewrite the poem in prose form. Replace any words you do not understand with a synonym. Does reading the poem in prose help you to better understand its meaning? Explain.

_____

_____

_____

_____

_____

Grammar Check

3. Change the punctuation in the sentences below to create a different mood. Rewrite the new sentences and explain the change in mood.

How can we go on living like this? With everything we have been through, we need to stay close friends.

_____

_____

_____

Speaking

4. Find another poem in the school library or on the Internet that uses animals as part of figurative language. Practice reading the poem aloud. Use the tone of your voice to show the mood as you read. Decide where you will pause and how you will adjust the volume and rate of your voice. Write some of your decisions below. When you are ready, read your poem to the class.

_____

_____

_____

_____

Listening

5. In a small group, choose one of the poems you found that uses animals as part of figurative language. Reread the poem together. Then write your ideas about the poem's message and how the figurative language helps to create this message. Afterward, discuss your ideas in the group. Listen carefully as your classmates share their thoughts and ideas even if they are different from yours.

_____

_____

_____

_____

A City of Words

Directions Write the answers to these questions. Use complete sentences.

Literary Terms

1. Think of a book you have recently read or a movie you have seen. Identify the protagonist and antagonist of the story on the lines below. Describe the conflict between the two.

_____

_____

_____

_____

Reading on Your Own

2. As you read, identify the different emotions that Rodriguez feels. How many of the emotions have you also felt in your conflicts with your family or friends? Explain.

_____

_____

_____

Grammar Check

3. Rewrite the following sentence, adding contractions where possible.

We do not want to go to the store; it is crowded on Saturday mornings, and we are not ready to battle the mass of people.

_____

_____

_____

Speaking

4. Consider what the author learns about relationships and languages as he gets older. What important lessons have you learned as you have grown older? Choose one lesson and describe it briefly below. Then explain what you have learned to the class, including specific details to support what you have learned.

_____

_____

_____

_____

_____

_____

_____

Listening

5. Listen carefully as each student explains the lesson that he or she has learned. Which lessons, mentioned by your peers, have you also learned as you have grown? Explain.

_____

_____

_____

_____

_____

Poems by Lucille Clifton

Directions Write the answers to these questions. Use complete sentences.

Literary Terms

1. Circle which of the following is *not* a quality of a free verse poem.

   A uses actual speech patterns

   B uses strict rhyming pattern

   C has irregular line length

   D has some kind of rhythm

Reading on Your Own

2. Choose one of Lucille Clifton's poems. Write one or two sentences to tell the main idea of the poem.

   _____

   _____

   _____

   _____

   _____

Grammar Check

Correct each sentence so that it is a complete thought and has a subject and a predicate. Add correct punctuation and capitalization. Rewrite each corrected sentence below.

3. getting ready to pick up jim and then flying out to new york city together

   _____

   _____

   _____

   _____

4. she watched the people passing her a woman with her dog a man talking on a cell phone a child chasing an ice cream truck

   _____

   _____

   _____

   _____

   _____

   _____

   _____

Speaking and Listening

5. Find another poem by Lucille Clifton in the school library or on the Internet. How does the poem fit the style you see in "morning mirror" and "my dream about the poet"? Are there differences? Write your observations below. Afterward, meet with a small group and discuss Clifton's style. Read your poem aloud to your group and then discuss your observations. Listen to decide how your group members' poems compare or contrast to your observations about Clifton's style.

   _____

   _____

   _____

   _____

   _____

Eleven

Directions Write the answers to these questions. Use complete sentences.

Literary Terms

1. What effect do you think exaggeration has on the reader? Explain using examples.

_____

_____

_____

_____

_____

Reading on Your Own

2. Before reading the story, what do you remember about being 11 years old? How did you react to conflict or difficult times? Explain.

_____

_____

_____

_____

_____

Grammar Check

Rewrite each of the following sentence fragments so that they are complete sentences.

3. Went to school to see the play

_____

_____

4. After we ate lunch on the beach

_____

_____

Speaking and Listening

5. How would you react if you were in Rachel's situation? Write your ideas below. Then form a small group and create a skit about this reaction. Use the same characters as the story. Perform the skit with group members playing the roles of Mrs. Price, Sylvia Saldívar, Phyllis Lopez, and Rachel. As you listen to other groups perform, how many groups had Rachel act the same way as your group?

_____

_____

_____

_____

_____

_____

_____

_____

_____

_____

_____

_____

The Starfish

Directions Write the answers to these questions. Use complete sentences.

Literary Terms

1. Which type of poem do you enjoy reading
   more: a prose poem or a free verse poem?
   Explain.

   _____

   _____

   _____

   _____

   _____

   _____

Reading on Your Own

2. Find another prose poem. As you read this
   poem, complete a Sequence Chain (described
   in Appendix A). How easy was it to complete
   the Sequence Chain? How does it compare to
   creating a Sequence Chain for other poems in
   this unit such as "A Simile" or "morning
   mirror"?

   _____

   _____

   _____

   _____

   _____

Grammar Check

Change the nouns in the following sentences
so that they are plural. Rewrite each sentence
below.

3. We took the child to the park to read her a
   story.

   _____

   _____

4. The sheep grazed in the field by the house.

   _____

   _____

Speaking and Listening

5. Read the last paragraph of "The Starfish"
   aloud. On another sheet of paper, rewrite the
   final paragraph in the form of a traditional
   poem. Decide where line breaks need to be
   inserted to create an effect. Afterward, read
   your work to a partner. As you listen to your
   partner's poem, how are choices in line breaks
   similar? How are they different? How do the
   line break differences affect the mood?

   _____

   _____

   _____

   _____

   _____

   _____

My Father and Myself Facing the Sun

Directions Write the answers to these questions. Use complete sentences.

Literary Terms

1. Why do authors use allusions? What effect do they have on the readers? Explain.

_____

_____

_____

_____

_____

_____

_____

Reading on Your Own

2. Circle the letter of the answer that is *not* part of the setting described in the poem.

A dusk

B August

C mountains

D a lake

Grammar Check

3. Circle the gerunds in the following sentences:

After traveling to Florida, I realized how much I love swimming in the ocean. I am planning to return to the ocean soon.

Speaking

4. Find a poem that presents a setting where you would like to live or spend time. Write why you would like to spend time there below. Practice reading the poem, making sure you can pronounce all of the words correctly. When you feel confident, share the poem with your class. Then explain why you like the setting.

_____

_____

_____

_____

_____

Listening

5. What sounds would you most likely hear in the setting of the poem you chose? Find a recording of these sounds or create them yourself. Explain how you think the sounds add to the description of the setting.

_____

_____

_____

_____

_____

_____

American Literature

Passports to Understanding

Directions Write the answers to these questions. Use complete sentences.

Literary Terms

1. Consider how Maya Angelou's personal essay would be different if her purpose had been to entertain readers. What might Angelou have included in the essay if this were her purpose?

_____

_____

_____

_____

Reading on Your Own

2. After reading Maya Angelou's personal essay, do you think "Passports to Understanding" is a good title? What other titles would work well for this essay?

_____

_____

_____

_____

Grammar Check

3. On the lines below, write a sentence that contains both an infinitive and a prepositional phrase.

_____

_____

_____

_____

Speaking

4. Contact a foreign exchange student at your school. Think of some questions to ask him or her about what he or she has learned about American culture. Also ask how he or she has been able to share his or her culture with Americans. On the lines below, write a short paragraph telling what you learned.

_____

_____

_____

_____

_____

_____

_____

Listening

5. Listen to an audio recording of Maya Angelou reading "On the Pulse of Morning," her inauguration poem for President Clinton. What do you notice about Angelou's voice as she reads? Write your observations below.

_____

_____

_____

_____

_____

_____

The Hundred Secret Senses

Directions Write the answers to these questions. Use complete sentences.

Literary Terms

1. Think of a story you have recently read or a movie you have seen that has a flashback. Explain what the flashback reveals and how it helps the reader better understand what is happening in the story.

_____

_____

_____

_____

_____

_____

_____

_____

Reading on Your Own

2. As you read *The Hundred Secret Senses*, focus on Olivia, her mother, or her father. Think about how the dialogue or actions help to reveal the character's traits. Afterward, summarize the character's personality in one sentence.

_____

_____

_____

_____

_____

Grammar Check

For each of the following sentences, place the apostrophes where they belong to show correct possession. Rewrite each sentence below.

3. Sarahs cat clawed its way up the neighbors tree.

_____

_____

4. The mens schedule included visiting the companies factories and dining at Marys restaurant.

_____

_____

_____

Speaking and Listening

5. Locate a copy of the novel *The Hundred Secret Senses*. Find a passage that you think is descriptive and well written. Explain why you think it is well written below. Read the passage aloud to a partner. As you listen to your partner's passage, decide what details allow you to picture the moment. Together, discuss Tan's style and what makes each passage well written, remembering what you have learned about figurative language and imagery.

_____

_____

_____

_____

Papi Working

Directions Write the answers to these questions. Use complete sentences.

Literary Terms

1. Circle the letter of the answer that has an example of both alliteration and onomatopoeia.

   A The twigs in the forest cracked and popped as we stepped on them.

   B The man missed his mother after she was gone.

   C The old house moaned as if it had some ailing pain.

   D The large lion roared loudly when others entered his space.

Reading on Your Own

2. Choose one example of alliteration from "Papi Working." Rewrite the line in your own words so that it no longer uses alliteration. Which way do you think is more powerful? Explain.

   _____

   _____

   _____

   _____

Grammar Check

3. Write a sentence of your own that uses words or phrases that are not English. Use the notes included in "Papi Working" to find words, or use words you already know. Underline the non-English words in your sentence.

   _____

   _____

   _____

   _____

Speaking

4. After preparing a choral reading of "Papi Working," find another poem to read with a small group. Again, decide which lines should be read loudly or quietly and who will read each line. Write your decisions below. Afterward, perform your poem in front of the class.

   _____

   _____

   _____

   _____

   _____

   _____

Listening

5. As you listen to the groups' second choral readings, what improvements do you notice between the reading of "Papi Working" and this new poem? What areas still need improvement?

   _____

   _____

   _____

   _____

   _____

   _____

The Antelope Wife

Directions Write the answers to these questions. Use complete sentences.

Literary Terms

1. What are some of the character traits you feel Louise Erdrich would include if she were writing a story about you?

_____

_____

_____

_____

Reading on Your Own

2. As you read *The Antelope Wife*, to which character do you feel you can best relate? Explain.

_____

_____

_____

_____

Grammar Check

3. Punctuate the selection titles correctly in the following sentence. Rewrite the corrected sentence on the lines below.

Everyday Use is my favorite short story, but The Hundred Secret Senses is my favorite book.

_____

_____

_____

_____

Speaking

4. Pretend that you will be interviewing Miss Peace McKnight about her experience as a teacher. Write questions that you will ask based on what you know from the story. Practice asking and answering the questions with a partner.

_____

_____

_____

_____

_____

_____

_____

_____

Listening

5. Listen as your teacher tells the story of how he or she became a teacher and some of the experiences he or she has had. What are some similarities your teacher and Miss Peace McKnight have had? What are some differences?

_____

_____

_____

_____

September 11 Literature

Directions Write the answers to these questions. Use complete sentences.

Literary Terms

1. Cut out a news article from a newspaper or magazine. Identify the byline of the article. What news event is the article about?

_____
_____
_____
_____
_____

Reading on Your Own

2. Decide how well you predicted what the theme of the four selections about September 11, 2001 would be. What parts did you predict accurately? What are some things that you did not expect?

_____
_____
_____
_____

Grammar Check

3. Punctuate the following sentence correctly, keeping in mind the common uses for the colon. Rewrite the corrected sentence on the lines below.

We have several things to do before 530 pick up James, deposit a check in the bank, and pick up the dry cleaning.

_____
_____
_____

Speaking

4. Imagine that you have been asked to create a news report about a school activity. Perhaps it is a film festival, a basketball game, or a pep rally. Write your ideas for the activity below. Create a report, pretending you are there as the activity happens. Remember that you are reporting the sights and sounds around you as well as the facts. Do your best to keep your emotions and personal feelings out of the report. Present the report to the class as if the action is happening right in front of you.

_____
_____
_____
_____
_____
_____

Listening

5. Watch a few different news reports on television. What similarities do you notice about the way the reporters speak? How do they often begin and end their reports? What other similarities do you notice? Record your observations below.

_____
_____
_____
_____

Unit 7 Review

Directions Write the answers to these questions. Use complete sentences.

Literary Terms

1. Why is imagery so important to use in writing? Explain.

_____

_____

_____

_____

_____

Reading on Your Own

2. After reading over the events and themes that writers are focusing on today, predict what you think authors will be writing about 50 years from now. Explain the reasons for your predictions.

_____

_____

_____

_____

_____

Grammar Check

Earlier in the unit, you learned that a gerund is a verb that ends in *–ing* but is used as a noun. A participle also looks like a verb. It most often ends in *–ing* or *–ed*. Unlike a gerund, however, a participle acts like an adjective in a sentence. Identify the gerunds and participles used in each of the sentences in the next column. Write *P* for participle and *G* for gerund.

3. Walking through the aisles, she did not see the dress that she had thought of wearing to the prom.

_____

_____

_____

_____

4. The girl running five miles a day was too tired for swimming and boating with her friends.

_____

_____

_____

_____

Speaking and Listening

5. How do you think the Internet has affected the way people experience and read literature? Write your ideas below. Then discuss this topic with your classmates. Offer your observations, and then listen carefully when others speak so that you can respond.

_____

_____

_____

_____

_____